MODERN MATHS
MADE EASY

P J Lines BSc (Hons) MBA

STELLAR BOOKS

Published in 2020 by:

Stellar Books
1 Birchdale
Bowdon
Cheshire
WA14 2PW

W: www.stellarbooks.co.uk
E: info@stellarbooks.co.uk

ISBN: 978-191-0275283

Book designed by PJ Lines

Published and printed in the United Kingdom

The author asserts his moral rights to be identified as the author of his work.

Dedicated to the memory of

Mum

(Norma)

With love

Phil x

CONTENTS

Fractions can be tricky, but we need to be comfortable working with them. This chapter shows the very simple Broken Window method.

This is a very simple method on how to deal with fractions; it shows just how "buzzwords" have crept into Arithmetic and this method; Stick Kiss Flip is a neat trick now used to divide fractions.

MODERN MATHS MADE EASY

About the Book

Mathematics (or numeracy) is a compulsory subject taught in schools from a very young age. However, many of us find it difficult and feel nowadays it has developed into a new language. The problem is made worse since our children are now taught new methods that are very different to how we were taught.

The new methods are not "bonkers," but they are different.

If your child comes home from school and asks for help with their homework be prepared to say: -

"What is A Number Line?"

"This is not how we learned long multiplication"

"I've never heard of Chunking"

In six easy to read chapters this book shows you how we learned Maths (back in the day) and then the same problem is translated into how your child is taught today.

Each chapter has worked examples and illustrations to help you navigate the new world of your child's Maths homework and understand the new methods they are now taught.

You will be introduced to a brand-new vocabulary of Maths such as the Number Line, the Multiplication Grid, the Chinese Box, The Broken Window and of course Chunking.

Oh! And by the way, you do not have to be a maths whizz to read this book as the examples are super easy to follow.

Chapter 1

THE NUMBER LINE

(Subtraction)

**Little Johnny has 12 doughnuts, he eats 7.
What does he have?**

Yes, that's right Type 2 Diabetes.

> "Dad, help me with this Maths question?"
> Squawked Sophie, my 9-year-old daughter.

Yuck, broccoli, boys and Maths!

"OK Sophie, read the question out to me"

Said I, thinking I can help.

Sophie continued:

"Use the Number Line to find the difference between 59 and 82"

Super smug Dad proceeds to show Sophie how this piece of Mathematical wizardry is achieved.

If you want to go into detail about how this is achieved, read on.

However, if you already know how to do double digit subtraction you can skip the next section.

Double Digit Subtraction

The word "difference" in Maths means subtraction or to put it another way; take the smaller number from the larger.

Mathematics has its own jargon and uses words that can sometimes confuse the student, these words include difference, product, dividend and quotient.

In my view they introduce unnecessary difficulty to the subject.

So, putting on the jargon buster hat.

Difference = Subtraction

Difference means subtract (or if you prefer take away).

Let us look at a simple example:

Find the difference between 2 and 7.
The answer is 5 or rather mathematically $7 - 2 = 5$.

Now back to the question.

Find the difference between 82 and 59.
Means $82 - 59 = $ Answer

A farmer takes 82 eggs to a market and sells 59 of them on the first day, how many eggs remain at the end of the first day.

We set the problem out in vertical columns.

$$
\begin{array}{r}
8\ 2 \\
-\ 5\ 9 \\
\hline
\text{Answer}
\end{array}
$$

8 2   Eggs at start of Day 1
- 5 9   Eggs sold on Day 1
Answer   Eggs remaining at the end of Day 1

Place Values – Or - Tens & Units

It might be helpful to understand the vertical columns when adding and subtracting double-digit or triple-digit numbers. These are called place values. In the number 82 the 8 is "placed" in the 10 (Tens) column and the 2 is "placed" in the 1s (Unit) column.

```
        T      U
  _     8      2
        5      9
```

The   U   Stands for Units or 1's.
The   T   Stands for Tens or 10's

82 is made up of two columns

In the T (tens) Column   We have 8 lots of 10 = 80   (8 x 10)
In the U (units) Column   We have 2 lots of 1 = 2   (2 x 1)

Similarly, for 59

If we had a three-digit number then it would be Hundreds, Tens and Units. And a four-digit number would be 1000's and so on.

There are 365 days in a year.

Written into columns this is: -

```
H      T      U
3      6      5
```

$$3 \times 100 = 300$$
$$6 \times 10 = 60$$
$$5 \times 1s = 5$$
$$365$$

Back to the Eggs

When adding and subtracting double (or more) digit numbers we always start with the units and move from right to left.

```
  T   U
  8   2
- 5   9
```

Starting on the Right-hand side and look at the two numbers in the Units column: the 2 and the 9.

We start with   2 – 9 =   [2 take away 9]

```
  T   U
  8   2
- 5   9
```

Well, we are not off to a great start, we cannot take 9 from 2. But if we borrow 10 eggs from a neighbour, we now have 12 eggs.

So, we will borrow 10 and give it to the 2 by putting a 1 in front of the 2 and it becomes 12.

```
  8  ¹2
- 5   9
      3
```

So now we have 12 take away 9 which equals 3.......

```
  8  ¹2
- 5   9
      3
```
Notice the 3 goes below the 9 but still in the Units column.

So far so good.

That 1 we put in front of the 2 to make it 12 is actually a ten (10) which we have borrowed from the 8 (Or 80) in 82.

You may be wondering why I have put a line through the 8

The 1 (10) we borrowed from the 8 (80) must be accounted for and therefore the 8 (80) now becomes a 7 (70).

Therefore, we cross out the 8 and replace with a 7.

```
    ⁷8̶  ¹2
  -  5   9
        3
```

Now we move to the left-hand column and instead of 8 take away 5 it is now 7 take away 5 which is 2.

^{7}8	^{1}2	Eggs at start of Day 1
- 5	9	Eggs sold during Day 1
2	3	Eggs at the end of Day 1

Therefore 82 – 59 = 23

Now then, is this correct?

We can check by adding the Answer (23) to the bottom number (59) If they add up to the top number then it is correct... 23 + 59 = 82

Super smug Dad has now shown Sophie how to perform the subtraction of two double digit numbers...ta dah.

However, there is still a problem.

"Dad the teacher said we had to use the Number Line Method"

The Number Line

This is a number line.

Hmm...,
Number Line
Fascinating

So, how does the number line method work then?

We place the larger number (82) on the right-hand side of the line and the smaller number on the left (59)

59   82

The number line is a bit like a ruler; so, we treat it like a 30cm ruler.

And for you really old gits 30cm is 12 inches.

"I've got Blue Monday by New Order on 30cm single" - Said No-one ever.

We need to find the difference (OR distance) between 59 and 82.

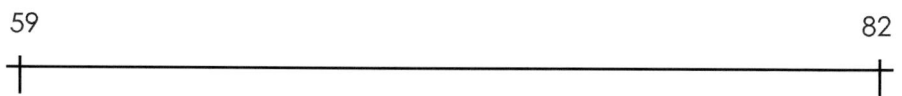

Next, we add in some milestones on this journey between 59 and 82, these milestones (numbers) will be multiples of 10 (i.e. numbers ending in a 0) between 59 and 82.

Which are obviously 60, 70 and 80

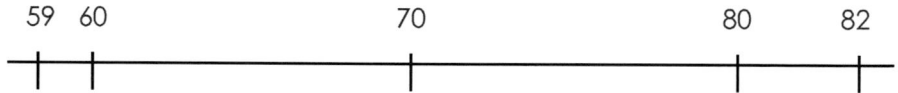

The number line is beginning to take shape and we can SEE the difference between 59 and 82...

Think of the numbers on the line as milestones on a journey.

Even if we do not yet know the difference between 59 and 82, we can **NOW** actually see or at least visualize the difference.

We essentially take a walk from Milestone 59 through to Milestone 82.

We can "measure" or add up the distances between the numbers; 59 and 82.

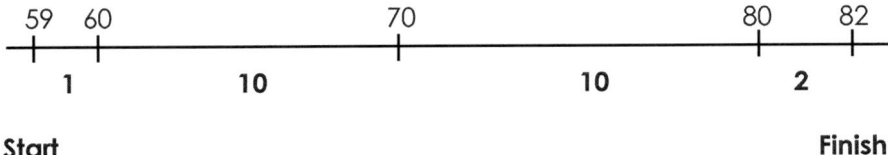

The numbers below the line are the "difference" between the two numbers immediately above them.

The difference (or step) between 59 and 60 is	1
The difference (or step) between 60 and 70 is	10
The difference (or step) between 70 and 80 is	10
The difference (or step) between 80 and 82 is	2

Add up the distances between the numbers: **23**

Or simply: **1 + 10 + 10 + 2 = 23**

The number line shows the **DIFFERENCE** between 59 and 82 is 23.

From initially being critical of the Number Line method I have become a fan of its visual appeal meaning students can **SEE** the difference between two numbers.

Summary

The number line gets two enthusiastic thumbs up from me.

The method works very well for young children coming to terms with Arithmetic.

I do not think it should ever replace the formal method, which uses place values (tens and units).

However, the number line is perfect for children who express a preference for visual learning. It is perfect for pencil and rough paper since the line does not need to be drawn to scale.

The fact that the line becomes a journey on a ruler that you can actually "see" and count between the numbers gives it credibility and a visual sense of purpose.

Ok put the book away, go and help your kid subtract two numbers and I will see you again when we need to multiply two numbers.

And if you are up for a challenge then here are two questions for you.

Use the Number Line to work these problems.

Q1:   Ramona has saved £72 and spends £45 on a new outfit, how much does she have left?

Q2:   Marita has a budget of £ 271 to spend on groceries each week, she spends £197 how much remains?

Answers at the back of the book.

Chapter 2

THE MULTIPLICATION GRID
(Long Multiplication)

A talking sheepdog gets all the sheep into the pen for the farmer. She comes back and says: -

"Okay, chief – all 40 sheep have been accounted for."

The farmer says, "But I've only got 36!"
The sheepdog replies, "I know, I rounded them up."

Back in the day we had to multiply two large numbers using a method known as long multiplication.

If you recall; the process of Long Multiplication was life threateningly dull.

I think I would rather pick a fight than learn long multiplication as it is such a long and tedious process. It is as painful as watching Miranda (Hart) the box set while undergoing root canal treatment without any anaesthetic.

Anyone having to learn Long Multiplication nowadays has my deepest sympathy.

However, that said we do need to know how to multiply two numbers together as we discover when we meet our next character: Farmer Gilly.

Farmer Gilly's Apples

Meet Farmer Gilly, obviously worried her post Brexit EU farming subsidies have potentially been kyboshed but nevertheless she cracks on with her apple harvest. After all, during the Covid 19 pandemic people are doing more home cooking so Apple Pies for Sunday pudding then.

Farmer Gilly needs to gather apples from her orchard, so she employs some students from the local high school. They will work from 7am to 4pm with an hour off for lunch, Facebook, twitter, snapchat and Instagram.

"Yeah good luck with that Gilly"

She knows that each full basket contains 58 apples and the students manage to fill 32 baskets.

Question: How many apples do they collect in total?

Answer: 32 baskets x 58 apples per basket = 1856.

Liz Truss (former UK Schools Minister) said calculators should be banned in primary schools. She has a point; the UK is 18th in the league table of developed nations for Maths.

However, it is not all bad news, the UK scores highly in teenage pregnancies when compared to many developed countries.

Broken Britain eh!

Anyway, back to the less controversial issue of calculators.

Is it a good idea to deny children the use of a calculator that is universally accessible on a mobile phone, tablet and laptop?

I will let the debate rage amongst the technophobes, Daily Mail readers, luddites and the intellectuals.

I am a pragmatist; I think students should use calculators but prior to reaching for the battery operated six shooter; students should have an appreciation of what the answer SHOULD be before they punch in the numbers. We all should be able to work out a reasonable estimate of the answer.

Recapping, there are 58 apples per basket and 32 full baskets.
So roughly how many apples should there be in the count.

Actual	Estimate	
58	60	[58 is almost 60]
32	30	[32 is almost 30]

We multiply 30 x 60 which is 3 x 6 then add the two zeros (0).
30 x 60 = 1800...

The actual count should be close to 1800.

In fact, 1800 is a pretty good estimate of 32 x 58.

Now I am sure I am not the only one in the UK with "sausage finger syndrome" when it comes to tapping in the wrong values into a calculator. And of course, who amongst us has not sent an embarrassing text whilst a bit squiffy.

Anyway, back to the apples, if (like me) you often punch in the wrong numbers or leave a digit out or add too many then errors will occur. There is a temptation to trust the calculator implicitly.

58 x 32 = 1856   [Seems straight forward enough]

However if instead (by accident) they put in: -

5 x 32 = 160   [A reluctant 8 that refuses to work]

or

58 x 320 = 18,560   [An extra zero after the 2]

If the answer comes out as 160 or 18,560 then there is a possibility, they will accept the answer without question. Yes, farmer Gilly there should be 18,560 apples.

If the students know the approximate answer is 1800 then either of these two numbers should be dismissed.

In my opinion the calculator should be used to confirm the correct answer (1856) only AFTER they have come up with a good estimate (1800).

Dad proceeds to show Sophie how long multiplication works.

Long Multiplication:

```
        3 2          Baskets filled.
  x      5 8         Apples per basket
        2 5 6
      1 6 0 0
      1 8 5 6        Total Number of Apples
```

If you want to see in more detail how Long Multiplication is achieved, then the method is shown at the end of this chapter.

Once again Dad has shown his daughter how to calculate the correct number of apples that Farmer Gilly's fruit pickers have managed to gather from the orchard.

But *"Ohhhh **noooo"*** that's not good enough, you need to find the number of apples collected using the grid method.

The Multiplication Grid Method

The Multiplication Grid is an alternative to long multiplication and quite frankly makes the multiplication process of two numbers a lot easier.

This method is now widely taught in schools especially for younger kids until they learn how to multiply together two, three and four digit numbers.

Why the change in method?

Question: Do you really need to know the nuts and bolts of the process to understand it properly?

Answer: The purists amongst us would scream YES.

However, ask yourself this question.

Do you need to understand how an internal combustion engine works in order to drive a car?

Do you need to know the inner workings of how a petrol engine with pistons, valves and cylinders operate in order to drive a car?

The answer is an unequivocal No. You do not need to be a car mechanic to be able drive a car. The same logic applies here.

The Grid Method is based on the idea of splitting the numbers being multiplied, into their component parts which in this case is the tens and units. Let us return to Farmer Gilly and her students.

32 baskets have been filled and each basket contains 58 apples, how many apples does Farmer Gilly have?

Place Values

"Oh no not these again we did these in Chapter One with the Number Line."

Well as much as I would like you to read this book, cover to cover (and tell 100s of people) I suspect people will read it in chapters like a recipe book.

If you recall doing the columns of numbers; Hundreds, Tens and Units then you will understand place values.

We split the two numbers using their place values. Our numbers (58 and 32) are only two digits so we need two columns: tens (T) and units or ones (U).

T U

5 8   is   50 or 5 tens [10s]   plus 8 units [1's]

3 2   is   30 or 3 tens [10s]   plus 2 units [1's]

We draw a 9-way grid (3 Columns by 3 Rows)

Fill in the Grid as follows:

On the first row of the Grid put in 50 and 8 (rows go across)

On the first column of the Grid put in 30 and 2 (columns go down)

I have put 58 x 32 in the top left cell just to remind us of the question.

58 x 32 =	50	8
30		
2		

NB: It does not matter if you put 32 across the top and 58 down.

You will now see 4 empty boxes. I have labelled them A B C and D

58 x 32 =	50	8
30	A	B
2	C	D

We fill in the squares (A B C and D) with the multiplication of the two numbers that head the row and the column.

58 x 32 =	50	8
30	30 x 50 = _A_	8 x 30 = _B_
2	50 x 2 = _C_	8 x 2 = _D_

Fill in the Answers to the 4 multiplications.

58 x 32 =	50	8
30	1500 _A_	240 _B_
2	100 _C_	16 _D_

There is an assumption here that the child understands that 8 x 30 is the same as 8 x 3 but with an extra 0 to allow for the 30 so 8 x 30 = 240.

And 50 x 30 is the same as 5 x 3 = 15, then add two more zeros = 1500.

There is also an assumption that your child knows their times tables. Kids must learn their times tables, no discussion, no debate.

Then we add up the numbers in the four boxes: -

Th	Hu	Te	Un	[Thousands Hundreds Tens Units]
1	5	0	0	Box A
	2	4	0	Box B
	1	0	0	Box C
		1	6	Box D
1	8	5	6	

I quite like the simplicity of the Grid Method ....

The grid method breaks down a complex problem into simpler and easier to manage problems.

The grid allows the student to see how the process works.

Initially I was a bit sceptical of the Grid Method but I really bang the drum for it now, I think it is a fabulous method and is so much simpler to see what is going on and easier to find out where an error has occurred. If you do make a mistake then you go back to the rogue cell within the grid, correct it and make good on your calculation.

Unlike Long Multiplication where if you make an error you must start from scratch. The grid allows you to see where you are going.

Read on if you have the need to refresh your memory on how Long Multiplication works.

Long Multiplication

Step 1

```
¹3 2          Baskets filled
  5 8          Apples per basket
```

Start on the right and side and multiply the two most right-hand numbers
2 x 8 = 16

Put the 6 (from the 16) under the 8 and put the 1 (from the 16) above the 3 as shown by ¹3.

Step 2

```
      ¹ 3 2
   x    5 8
      2 5 6
```

Then multiply the 8 (from the 58) by the 3 (in the 32) and add the little 1.

3 x 8 + 1 = 24 + 1 − 25.

Put the 25 to the left of the 6 as shown by 256.

You have now multiplied 8 x 32 – Congratulations!

Step 3

```
        3 2
    x   5 8
      2 5 6
          0
```

Put a zero (0) under the 6 as shown.

Why the zero?

We just multiplied 32 x 8 and got 256. We now multiply 50 by 32 so it's easier if we put a 0 as shown and multiply 5 x 32 because any whole number multiplied by 10 ends in a zero.

Step 4

```
      ¹3 2
   x   5 8
     2 5 6
       0 0
```

Then multiply the **5** (from the 58) by the **2** (from the 32).

5 x 2 = **10**

Put the **0** (from the answer 10) to the left of the 0 from **Step 3**.

Put the 1 (from the answer 10) above the 13.

Step 5

```
    ¹  3 2
   x   5 8
     2 5 6
   1 6 0 0
```

Then multiply the **5** (from the 58) by the **3** (from the 32) then add the 1 from the ¹ **3**

5 x 3 + 1 = 15 + 1 = 16

Put the 16 to the left of the 0 0.

Step 6

```
       3 2
   x   5 8
     2 5 6
   1 6 0 0 +
   1 8 5 6
```

Then add the bottom two rows together 256 + 1600 = 1856

"Phew, that was exhausting, gimme the grid method any day".

Use the Multiplication Grid to find the answers to these problems.

Q 1:   A restaurant has 92 covers each evening and the average diner spends £ 65 a head, calculate the amount of money collected when the restaurant closes?

Q2:   In the UK, the prison population is 82,458 and it costs £ 22,548 pa. Calculate the total prison budget.

Answers at the back of the book.

Chapter 3

THE CHINESE BOX
(Long Multiplication)

A mathematician and an engineer are sitting in a bar looking at a gorgeous young man.

The mathematician sighs. *"I'd like to talk to him, but the rule is I have to walk half the distance between where we are and where he is, then half of the distance that remains, then half of that distance again, and so on. So, there will always be some small distance between us." 64 paces then 32 paces which becomes 16, then 8 then 4 then 2 then 1 then 0.5 pace then 0.25 then smaller and smaller but never ever actually getting to zero"*

The engineer gets up and she starts walking towards him. *"Where are you going?"* said the Mathematician," *I just told you based on our walking patterns the distance will never be zero"*

The engineer responds: *"Ah, well, I estimate I can get close enough for practical purposes, I bet 3cm should be close enough to play tonsil hockey".*

Now The Chinese Box is seriously spooky, I have no idea how it works but I had the pleasure of watching Harry my 13-year-old son do his Maths homework using The Chinese Box Method.

If you have just read Chapter Two and are now familiar with The Multiplication Grid, then you can now multiply two double digit numbers.

This eponymously named method is another alternative to the laborious task of long multiplication. Let us return to Farmer Gilly with her 32 baskets of apples with 58 apples per basket.

How many apples were collected by Farmer Gilly's little helpers this time using the Chinese Box?

We split the numbers in a 3 by 3 grid as below.

5	8	58 x 32 =
		3
		2

The difference here is that we head the columns with 5 and 8 Not 50 and 8 and the rows are headed 3 and 2 not 30 and 2.

Then we add in some diagonals as shown in the four answer boxes.

5	8	58 x 32 =
		3
		2

Then we multiply the number pairs and put the double-digit answer in the boxes BUT either side of the diagonal.

Because we are multiplying with 5, 8, 3 and 2 the Maths is even simpler as we are now multiplying single digits from the good old 12 times tables.

In this example:

5 x 3 = 15	8 x 3 = 24
5 x 2 = 10	8 x 2 = 16

Look how we place the 1 and 5 in the 15 either side of the diagonal arrow. Similarly, for the 24, 10 and 16.

5	8	58 x 32 =
1 5 (5 x 3 = 15)	2 4 (8 x 3 = 24)	3
1 0 (5 x 2 = 10)	1 6 (8 x 2 = 16)	2

OK so where does that leave us?

We now have the 4 boxes filled in with four two-digit numbers either side of four diagonal lines. It looks very pretty but what happens next.

We extend each diagonal to emerge outside of the grid on the left side.

In addition, I have also placed four speech bubbles each showing the four place values: thousands, hundreds, tens and units.

The four columns depicting thousands, hundreds, tens and units are now in diagonal columns from top left to bottom right.

We will now add up the diagonal columns.

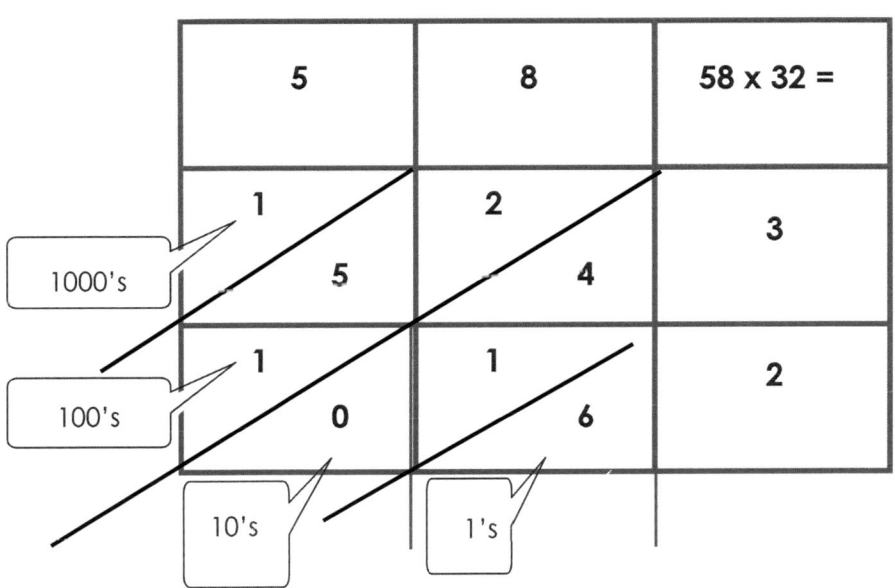

Adding up the diagonals

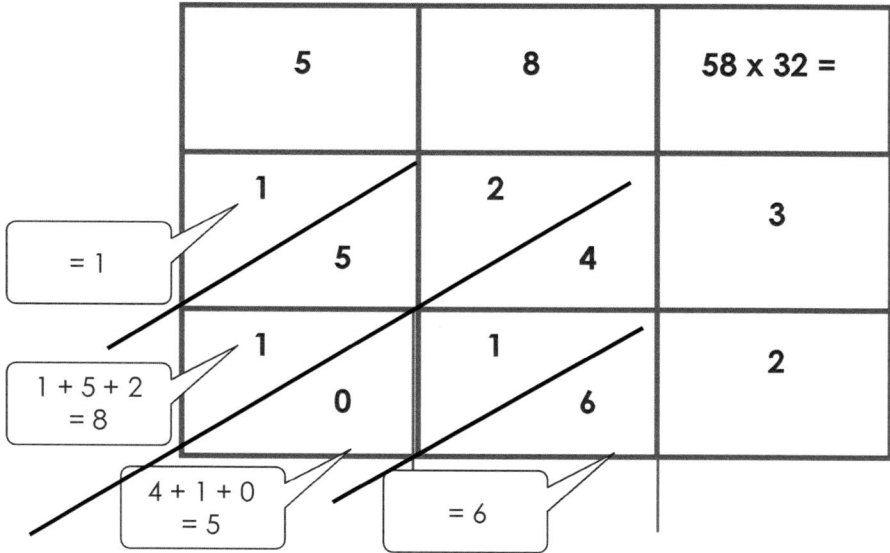

Starting from the top left reading the answers from the speech bubbles left to right the answer is 1856.

A more difficult one

OK so now we know the Chinese Multiplication Box is weird and I am still not sure how it works but we just need to accept the fact that it does work.

The questions will obviously become more complicated.

Here we see the completed box for 327 x 586....

The diagonals are all filled in from top right to bottom left.

Each cell has been completed with the product (answer) of the two numbers. As you can see, we need a much bigger grid and there are now six diagonal channels.

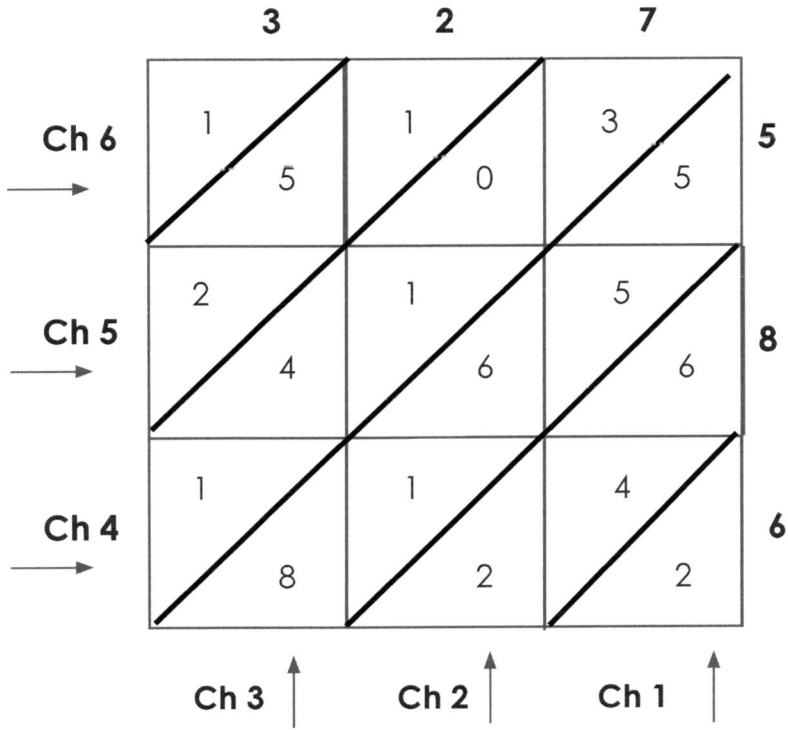

The 1st diagonal channel (Headed by 6 on the outside)

There is ONLY one number in the bottom right hand diagonal channel and it is 2.

So, we put the 2 as shown.

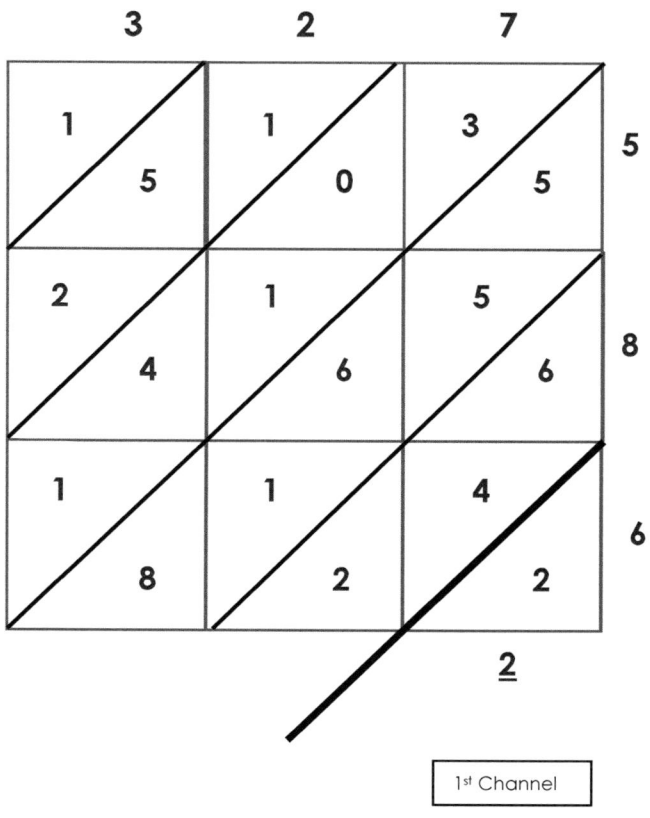

1st Channel

The 2nd diagonal channel (Headed by 8 on the outside)

There are three numbers in the 2nd channel (6, 4 and 2)

So we add them up and we get 6 + 4 + 2 = 12

We put the 2 from the 12 at the bottom of the 2nd channel and carry the 1 (boxed) into the 3rd channel.

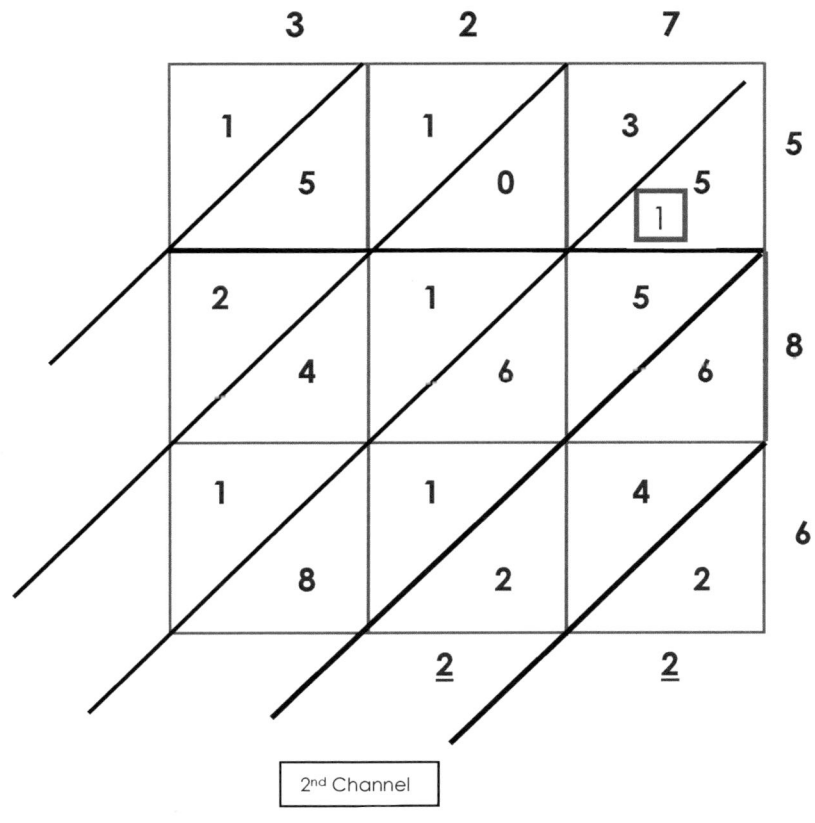

2nd Channel

43

The 3rd diagonal channel (Headed by 5 on the side)

There are five numbers in the 3ʳᵈ channel (5, 5, 6, 1 and 8) plus the $\boxed{1}$ in the box carried forward from the 2ⁿᵈ channel.

So, we add them up and we get $\qquad 5 + 5 + 6 + 1 + 8 + \boxed{1} = 26$

We put the 6 from the 26 at the bottom of the 3ʳᵈ channel and carry the 2 from the 26 and place this is in the box $\boxed{2}$ in the 4ᵗʰ channel, headed by the 7 at the top.

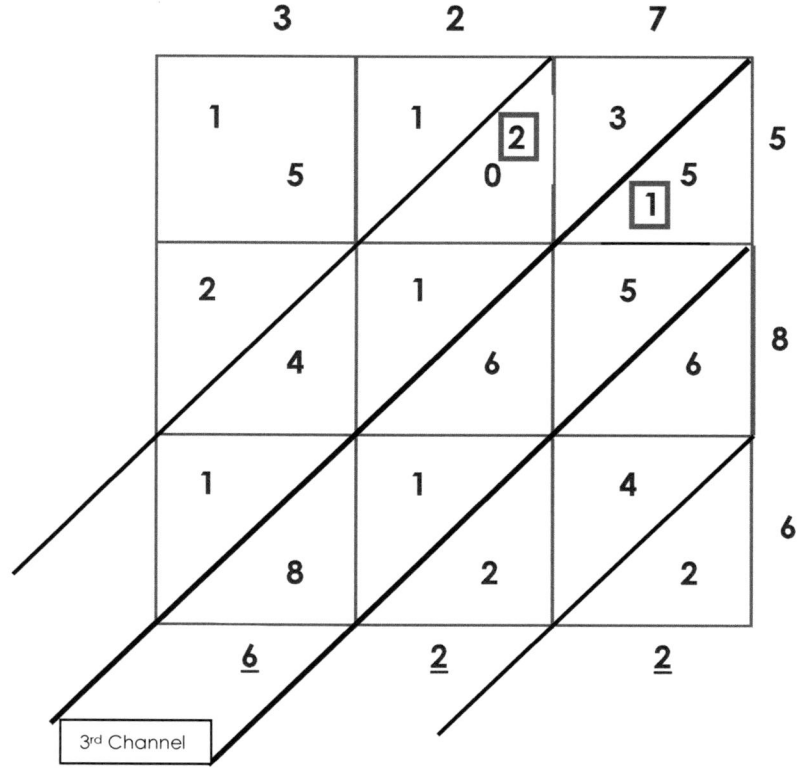

3rd Channel

44

The 4th diagonal channel (Headed by 7 on the outside)

There are five numbers in the 4th channel (3, 0, 1, 4 and 1) plus the 2 in the box carried forward from the 3rd channel.

So, we add them up and we get   3 + 0 + 1 + 4 + 1 + 2 = 11

We put the right hand 1 from the 11 at the side of the 4th channel and carry the left hand 1 from the 11 and put it in a box 1 and put it in the 5th channel headed with a 2.

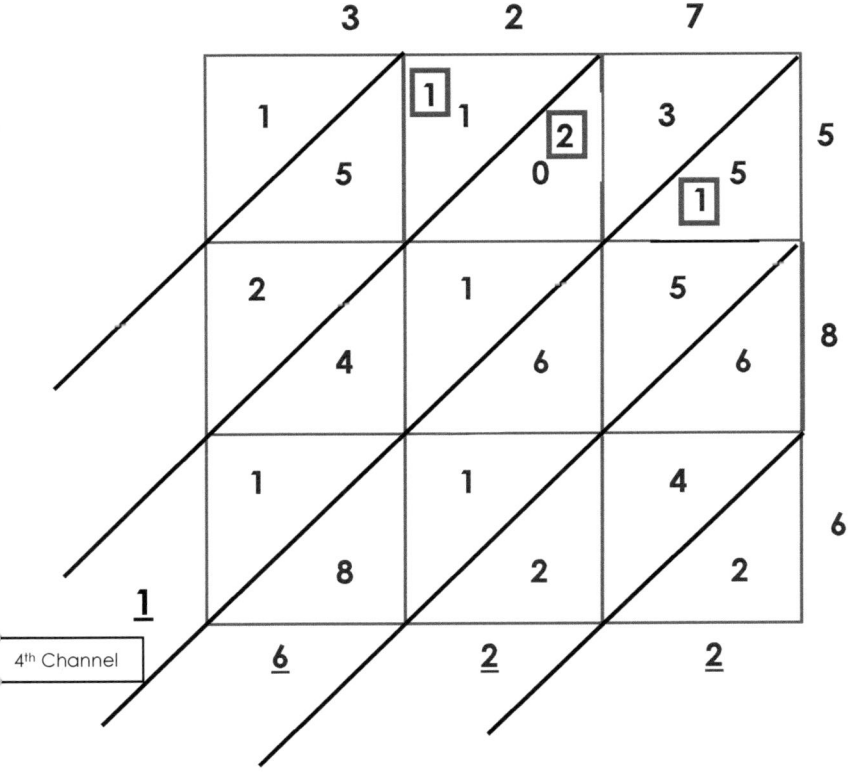

The 5th diagonal channel (Headed by 2 on the outside)

There are three numbers in the 5th channel (1, 5 and 2) plus the $\boxed{1}$ in the box from the 4th channel.

So, we add the numbers up in the 5th channel and we get

$1 + 5 + 2 + \boxed{1} = 9$

We put the 9 at the side of the 5th channel and there is nothing to carry to the 6th channel.

Channel 6 (Headed by 3 on outside) has a solitary 1 in it to add up

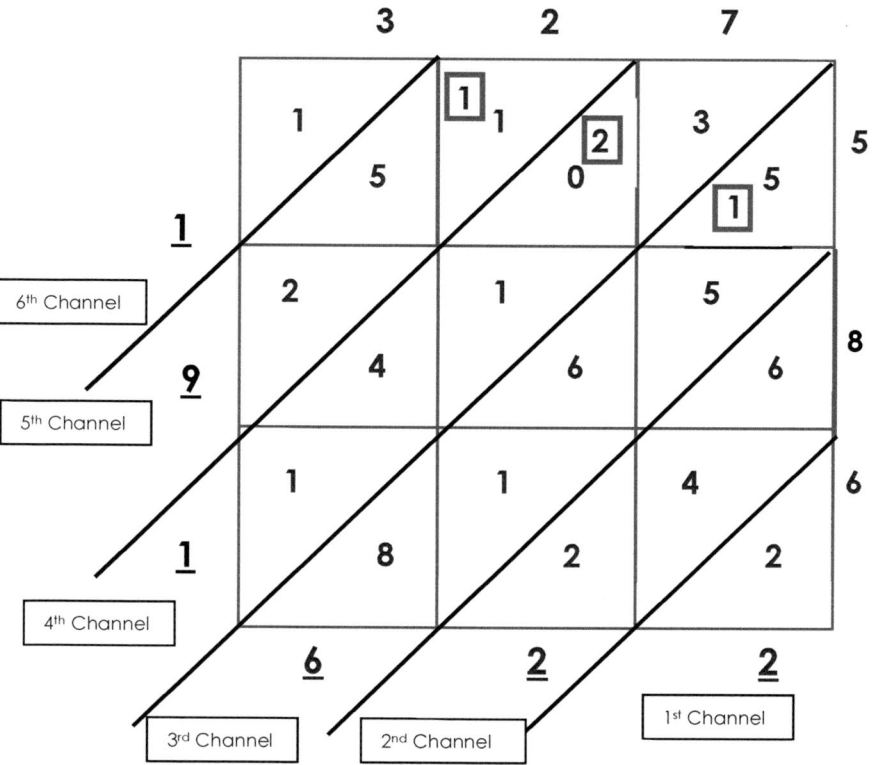

Reading left to right down and round the corner the number reads 191,622

Therefore   327 x 586 = 191,622

Summary

So, what do we make of the Chinese method?

      1)   It works

      2)   It is kind of fun and a bit quirky.

      3)   It is a bit odd to begin with.

      4)   The Maths is much simpler

      5)   It is far quicker than the grid method

      6)   It is easier to teach and learn.

I like it.

And before anyone says I do not like these new modern methods we need to keep to the traditional long multiplication method that has been going around for hundreds of years.

Well this method dates back to the late Chinese Shang Dynasty around the 11th century BC some 3000 years ago.

In the next chapter we will be looking at how Long Division is now taught by using the Chunking Method.

Use the Chinese Box method to work out these problems.

Q1:   An average portion contains 38 chips and each chip contains 29 calories. Calculate the amount of calories consumed by eating one portion of chips.

Q2:   The average salary of a teacher in the UK is £ 27,578 pa and there are approximately 32,295 teachers calculate annual wage budget.

Answers at the back of the book.

Chapter 4

CHUNKING
(Long Division)

Q: How do you eat an elephant?

A: One chunk at a time.

When did you last do long division?

Do you remember how tough it was?

A new method has been developed called CHUNKING which is based on the mental process involved when we do long division in our head.

'Chunking is the devil's work'

This method of dividing a larger number by a smaller number is now widely taught in our schools.

This is one definition: -

"Chunking is the repeated subtraction of the divisor and multiples of the divisor - in other words, working out how many groups of a number fit into another number. The purpose of chunking is for students to be able to think about the relationship between multiplication and division"

Are you clear about this?

Well I certainly am not, that is an awful definition.

The jury is out on this and I cannot come to a clear decision as to whether I prefer Chunking over Long Division. I think, on balance I do not like this method, but it has some merits.

For:

Chunking is easier and maybe more appealing for some pupils who prefer a step by step approach.

It is a good method for those children who are still learning their Times Tables and realise that say seven goes into 59, eight times with three left over (remaining).   Or $59 \div 7 = 8$ remainder 3.

Against:

Chunking is very long winded and there are many steps (albeit easier steps) for errors to occur.

It also relies on some educated guess work and guessing is never good in a precise science like Maths. Guessing is not to be confused with estimating.

The idea behind chunking is to break down one complicated very long division into several simpler ones.

The beauty of Maths is that we can always look at an example.

Grandad wishes to gift £ 2640 to his six grandchildren.

How much does each grandchild receive?

So that is   £ 2640 $\div$ 6

Each child receives   £ 440

According to the calculator the answer is 440 but we need to arrive at this answer without using a calculator.

Death of Calculators

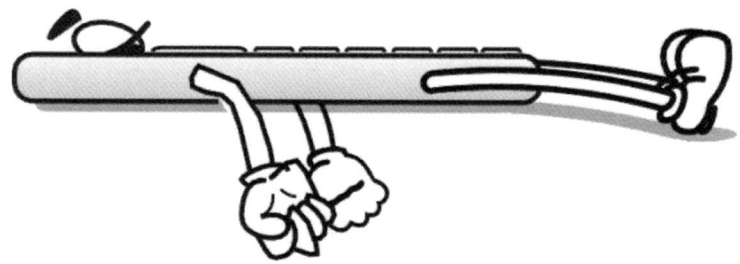

It was announced in 2012 that calculators in primary school would be banned. Back then Michael Gove was Minister for Education and we were in the EU and we did not have Covid 19 lockdown so the world may have changed somewhat,

The fact that every single mobile phone is pretty much a watch, alarm clock, video camera, internet terminal, text machine, social media vehicle, portable game station **and a calculator** then good luck with the ban.

Whether it is a good idea to deny children the technology they rely on is one thing but having a grasp of the numbers is VERY important.

Back to Grandad...

Short Division (The Bus Stop Method)

Let us remind ourselves how short division works, 2640 ÷ 6 is laid out as follows.

The bus stop method is to push the 6 into the bus stop where 2640 awaits.

$$6\overline{)2\ 6\ 4\ 0}$$
$$4$$

6 into 2 won't go so we do 6 into 26 which gives us an answer of 4 with 2 remainder.

26 ÷ 6 = 4 times and remainder 2.

The remainder 2 now goes in front of the 4 to become 24 so now its 6 into 24 which is another 4

$$6\overline{)2\ 6\ \overset{2}{4}\ 0}$$
$$4\ 4\ 0$$

Then 6 into the final zero (0) goes zero times.

£ 2640 divided by 6 equals 440 so each grand child receives £ 440

The Elements of a Division Question

Jargon alert again, more nonsense from our elite educators who seem to take obscene delight in making the subject more complicated than is necessary and causing more children to disengage from Maths.

The elements are called: -

1.   Quotient (the big number that is to be divided up)

[In this case Grandads gift - £2640)

2.   Divisor (the smaller number we are dividing by)

[The 6 grandchildren]

3.   Dividend (or in plain English the answer)

[The amount each grand child receives £ 440]

The reason why I have shown you the elements of the division is because they are referred to in the chunking method.

Chunking

As I have said earlier, I am not completely comfortable with this method.

My problem is that chunking is only practical for relatively small numbers, or at least small divisors, while long division is useful anytime. Also, there is too much flexibility in how chunking can be applied, and that has the effect that chunking relies on guesswork.

As a tutor I teach all methods and allow the students to choose.

Basically, you have a big number (quotient) say 2640 (Granddads gift) and you want to divide it by a smaller number (divisor) say 6 (the grand children).

As the name implies, we will divide the 2640 (quotient) into bite size digestible chunks.

We can accept that for most children (and most adults) that it is easy to multiply ANY number by 1, 2, 5, 10 and 100.

We are working with the divisor 6.

We are going to find "chunks" of 6.

So, the five easy multiples (chunks) of 6 that we should know.

1 x 6 = 6	1 chunk of 6	=	6
2 x 6 = 12	2 chunks of 6	=	12
5 x 6 = 30	5 chunks of 6	=	30
10 x 6 = 60	10 chunks of 6	=	60
100 x 6 = 600	100 chunks of 6	=	600

We know then, the five relatively easy multiples of 6 are 6, 12, 30, 60 & 600

These five numbers we identify as **Chunks** (of 6)

6   12   30   60   600

Now we take the chunks away from the quotient (big number) starting high and going lower.

Starting Point	2640	Chunks (of 6)
Take away the 1st chunk	- 600	**100**
Leaving	2040	
Take away a 2nd chunk	- 600	**100**
Leaving	1440	
Take away a 3rd chunk	- 600	**100**
Leaving	840	
Take away a 4th chunk	- 600	**100**
Leaving [We can't take 600 from 240]	240	
Take away a 5th chunk	- 60	**10**
Leaving	180	
Take away a 6th chunk	- 60	**10**
Leaving	120	
Take away a 7th chunk	- 60	**10**
Leaving	60	
Take away an 8th chunk	- 60	**10**
Leaving	0	
Once we have 0 left we stop.		**440**

These are our chunks; 6, 12, 30, 60, 600 that we take away from 2640.

Add up all the numbers on the right (the chunks) in bold: -

The numbers on the right (in Bold) are the multiples of 6 that give us the chunks.

100

100

100

100

10

10

10

10

440

So, 2640 divided by 6 = 440

Use the Chunking method to evaluate these problems.

Q1:   £ 1400 is to be shared between 8 people, how much does each person receive?

Q2:   Jane travels 408 miles in the car for 6 hours without a rest, calculate her average speed.

Hint: Speed = Distance ÷ Time

Answers at the back of the book.

Chapter 5

THE BROKEN WINDOW

(How to add and subtract fractions)

Did you know...

"5 out of every 3 people are c**p at fractions"

(Ken Dodd)

In this chapter we are going into the murky underworld of fractions.

You will learn about the following subjects that are all on the national curriculum.

Adding and Subtracting Fractions
Simplifying Fractions to their lowest forms.
Lowest Common Denominators (LCD)
Mixed Numbers

AND ta dah ! The Broken Window

Adding Fractions

When we add numbers its quite easy 3 + 5 = 8.

[Or at least it should be easy]

It is not quite as easy when we add fractions.

Let us look at a Common Mistake done by students Add ¼ + ⁵/₉

$$\frac{1}{4} \quad + \quad \frac{5}{9}$$

The student adds the top numbers together (1 + 5 = 6)

And the bottom numbers (4 + 9 = 13).

$$\frac{1}{4} \quad + \quad \frac{5}{9} \quad = \quad \frac{6}{13} \quad \text{Wrong Wrong Wrong}$$

This could not be more wrong!

Now some terms you will need to know:

Numerator (top number) – In this case 1

$$\frac{1}{4}$$

Denominator (bottom number) – In this case 4.

The answer is:

$$\frac{1}{4} \quad + \quad \frac{5}{9} \quad = \quad \frac{9 + 20}{36} \quad = \quad \frac{29}{36}$$

So how do you do this?

And how come one quarter plus five ninths is twenty nine over thirty six?

Lowest Common Multiple (LCM)

We need to know how to find the LCM when we add / subtract fractions.

If we need to add

$$\frac{1}{4} \quad + \quad \frac{5}{9} \quad = \quad \frac{\rule{2cm}{0.4pt}}{\text{LCM}}$$

We then need to find the LCM of the two denominators 4 and 9. So how do we find the LCM of 4 and 9. We need to look at ALL the multiples of 4 and 9.

In some books this is called LCD (Lowest Common Denominator) –

It is the same thing.

Essentially, we need to look at the 4 and 9 times tables.

1 x 4 = 4	1 x 9 = 9	
2 x 4 = 8	2 x 9 = 18	
3 x 4 = 12	3 x 9 = 27	Answers to right of
4 x 4 = 16	**4 x 9 = 36**	the equal (=) sign are
5 x 4 = 20	5 x 9 = 45	**MULTIPLES** of 4 and 9.
6 x 4 = 24	6 x 9 = 54	
7 x 4 = 28	7 x 9 = 63	We can see that 36
8 x 4 = 32	8 x 9 = 72	appears in BOTH lists.
9 x 4 = 36	9 x 9 = 81	
10 x 4 = 40	10 x 9 = 90	
11 x 4 = 44	11 x 9 = 99	
12 x 4 = 48	12 x 9 = 108	

Hopefully you can spot the multiple that appears in the answer column in both the 4 and 9 times table.

The (LCM) Lowest Common Multiple for 4 and 9 is 36.

We arrange the fractions as below: -

$$\frac{1}{4} \quad + \quad \frac{5}{9} \quad = \quad \frac{}{36}$$

Start with the 1st denominator on the left (4) and this divides into the LCM (36) exactly 9 times.

Then multiply this 9 by the numerator on the left (1) and we get 9.

Put the 9 as below followed by the plus sign (+).

$$\frac{1}{4} \quad + \quad \frac{5}{9} \quad = \quad \frac{9 +}{36}$$

Then we take the 2nd denominator (9) and divide this into the LCM (36) and it goes 4 times.

Then multiply this 4 by the second numerator (5) and we get 20.

Put this 20 as below.

$$\frac{1}{4} \quad + \quad \frac{5}{9} \quad = \quad \frac{9 + 20}{36}$$

Then add the 9 + 20.

$$\frac{1}{4} \quad + \quad \frac{5}{9} \quad = \quad \frac{9 + 20}{36} \quad = \quad \frac{29}{36}$$

Answer = 29 / 36

So instead of having 5/9 and 1/4 we have a fraction of 29/36.

Shall we do another?

Add

$$\frac{3}{4} \quad + \quad \frac{2}{3}$$

Find the LCM (Lowest Common Multiple) of 3 and 4.

X	3	4
1	3	4
2	6	8
3	9	**12**
4	**12**	16
5	15	20

The (LCM) Lowest Common Multiple of 3 and 4 is 12

Often (but not always) the LCM can be found by multiplying the denominators. The method is still the same.

That means 3 and 4 will BOTH go into 12 without any remainders.

We arrange as below: -

$$\frac{3}{4} \quad + \quad \frac{2}{3} \quad = \quad \frac{}{12}$$

Then we divide the 4 (1st denominator) into 12 (LCM) and see how many times it goes. Answer = 3.

Then times this 3 by the 3 (1st numerator) and we get 9.

$$\frac{3}{4} \quad + \quad \frac{2}{3} \quad = \quad \frac{9 +}{12}$$

Then we divide the 3 (2nd denominator) into the 12 (LCM) and see how many times it goes. Answer = 4

Then times this 4 by the 2 (2nd numerator) and we get 8.

$$\frac{3}{4} \quad + \quad \frac{2}{3} \quad = \quad \frac{9 + 8}{12} \quad = \quad \frac{17}{12}$$

Now that is odd, we have a funny looking fraction 17/12.

Seventeen over twelve, how does that work?

Normally with fractions the smaller number is on the top.

This is called an improper or top-heavy fraction.

Now, back in the old days a fraction such as 17/12 used to be called a vulgar fraction. Now the more polite term Improper Fraction is favoured.

Or more commonly known as Top Heavy.

A Vulgar Fraction   17 / 12

So back to the question

$$\frac{3}{4} \quad + \quad \frac{2}{3} \quad = \quad \frac{9 + 8}{12} \quad = \quad \frac{17}{12}$$

We have an answer that is an Improper Fraction 17/12.

This is because when we add 3/4 to 2/3 the answer is greater than 1, the answer will be 1 and a bit.

We must not leave the answer in this form 17/12.

How many times will denominator (12) go into numerator (17).

The answer is of course 1 and this is the whole number in the answer.

12 goes into 17 just once (1) and remainder 5. We out the remainder over the 12.

$$\frac{17}{12} \quad = \quad 1 \text{ and } 5/12$$

The answer is a MIXED number i.e. This consists of a whole Number 1 and a fraction of 5 / 12.

It is spoken as "one and five twelfths."   1 and 5/12

Recapping: -

$$\frac{3}{4} \quad + \quad \frac{2}{3} \quad = \quad \frac{9 + 8}{12} \quad = \quad \frac{17}{12}$$

1 and **$\frac{5}{12}$**

Let's recap we need to find the LCM or Lowest Common Multiple of the two denominators 4 & 3 which is 12.

Then we put 4 into 12 which give 3 then we times that by the numerator 3 which gives us 9 then add this to the 8 which we get from dividing the second denominator 3 into 12 which gives us 4 which we times by 2.

Then add 9 + 8 = 17 over 12.

Again, this is exhausting, long winded and way over the top.

Let's smash this method, break the glass window and use a different method.

The Broken Window Method

Do you remember the old Children's TV show called *Playschool* when they cut to a badly filmed sketch involving precocious children playing in a sandpit sharing sandwiches and being nice to each other?

It was probably the least interesting segment of the show for bored six-year olds and potentially the least realistic representation of kids, but it was preceded by the announcer saying:

"Well today children, WILL our story be told through the round window, the square window or will it be the arch window"

"Well today parents we are going to look through the Broken Window...."

Add one quarter plus five ninths.

$$\frac{1}{4} \quad + \quad \frac{5}{9}$$

You will never guess we build another grid (if you prefer a 9 - way table or 3 by 3).

We put the question in the top left corner then put the 1/4 as shown along the TOP ROW and the 5/9 down the LEFT COLUMN as shown.

1/4 + 5/9	1	4
5		
9		

We then break the middle window!

1/4 + 5/9	1	4
5	✕	
9		

We then fill in the three remaining cells with the product (product is jargon for multiplication or times) of the two numbers at the end of each column and row.

1/4 + 5/9	1	4
5	✕	4 x 5
9	1 x 9	4 x 9

Fill in the answers (shown in bold).

1/4 + 5/9	1	4
5		**20**
9	**9**	**36**

Now then we take the number in the bottom right hand corner (36)

And this will be the denominator for the answer   / 36

The numerator for the answer is found by adding the 9 and 20 = 29

The answer is 29 / 36…..

Answer = $\dfrac{9 + 20}{36}$ = $\dfrac{29}{36}$

How easy is that?

Ready for another?

If we need to add

$$\frac{3}{4} + \frac{5}{7}$$

3/4 + 5/7	3	4
5	✕	4 x 5
7	7 x 3	7 x 4

3/4 + 5/7	3	4
5	✕	20
7	21	28

Answer is $\dfrac{21 + 20}{28}$ = $\dfrac{41}{28}$

28 goes into 41 once (1) so we have a whole number 1 in our answer then 41-28 gives us the remainder which is 13.

The answer is   1 & 13/28

What about a harder one?

$$\frac{3}{4} \quad + \quad \frac{2}{3}$$

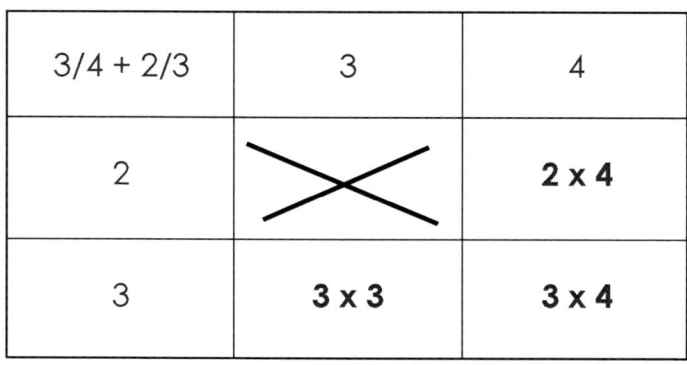

3/4 + 2/3	3	4
2		2 x 4
3	3 x 3	3 x 4

3/4 + 2/3	3	4
2		8
3	9	12

Answer is $\frac{9 + 8}{12}$ = $\frac{17}{12}$

12 goes into 17 once and remainder five then put the 5 over the 12.

That becomes 1 & 5/12.

Subtracting Fractions

Very similar process

$$\frac{3}{4} \quad - \quad \frac{1}{3}$$

3/4 - 1/3	3	4
1	✕	1 x 4
3	3 x 3	3 x 4

3/4 - 1/3	3	4
1	✕	4
3	9	12

Answer is $\quad \dfrac{9 - 4}{12} \quad = \quad \dfrac{5}{12}$

We still look at the diagonals but subtract the smaller from the larger.

There you have it, the Broken Window method – "Smashed it."

Use the Broken Window method to work out these two problems.

Q1:   3/4   +   5/7

Q2:   6/7   -   2/3

Answers at the back of the book

Chapter 6

STICK KISS FLIP

(How to multiply and divide fractions)

Q: Which British King invented fractions?

A: Richard the Third.

I would advise you to read Chapter 5 before reading Chapter 6 as some of the concepts covered with fractions are used here.

In Chapter 5 we learned how to: -

- Add and subtract fractions
- Simplify top heavy fractions
- Understand mixed numbers.

We will need some of these skills when we come to multiplying and dividing fractions.

In many ways this is easier than adding and subtracting as we do not have to find any Lowest Common Multiples, we do not have to break any windows nor build any grids.

Example 1

Multiply
$$\frac{3}{4} \quad \times \quad \frac{5}{7} \quad =$$

Arrange like this
$$\frac{3}{4} \quad \times \quad \frac{5}{7} \quad = \quad \frac{3 \times 5}{4 \times 7}$$

"The multiplication of fractions is NOT a problem it is
top times top and bottom times bottom"

As the rhyme says you multiply the numerators (3 x 5) and multiply the denominators (4 x 7).

So
$$\frac{3}{4} \quad \times \quad \frac{5}{7} \quad = \quad \frac{3 \times 5}{4 \times 7} \quad = \quad \frac{15}{28}$$

It is that simple.

Sometimes (like 15/28) that is the end as this is the answer.

BUT you may need to simplify the answer further.

Example 2

Multiply $\quad \dfrac{3}{4} \quad \times \quad \dfrac{2}{3} \quad = \quad \dfrac{3 \times 2}{4 \times 3} \quad = \quad \dfrac{6}{12}$

Therefore 3/4 x 2/3 = 6/12

We cannot leave the answer like this, we need to simplify 6/12.

$$\overset{\div 6}{\underset{\div 6}{\dfrac{6}{12}}} \quad = \quad \dfrac{1}{2} \qquad \text{(Divide numerator \& denominator by 6)}$$

So $\quad \dfrac{3}{4} \times \dfrac{2}{3} \quad = \quad \dfrac{3 \times 2}{4 \times 3} \quad = \quad \dfrac{6}{12} \quad = \quad \dfrac{1}{2}$

We have simplified the fraction 6/12 into its lowest form 1/2.

Example 3

Multiply $\dfrac{3}{10}$ x $\dfrac{20}{33}$ = $\dfrac{3 \times 20}{10 \times 33}$

We could multiply top by top and then bottom by bottom.

$\dfrac{3 \times 20}{10 \times 33}$ = $\dfrac{60}{330}$

We can cancel and simplify this.

$$\dfrac{3 \times 20}{10 \times 33}$$

We can see that 20 and 10 are BOTH divisible by 10.

And 33 and 3 are BOTH divisible by 3.

$$\dfrac{\overset{1}{3} \times \overset{2}{\cancel{20}}}{\underset{1}{\cancel{10}} \times \underset{11}{\cancel{33}}}$$

We divide 3 into 3 (numerator) and we cross out the 3 and put 1.
We divide 3 into 33 (denominator) we cross it out and put 11.

We divide 10 into 20 (numerator) and we cross out 20 and put 2.
We divide 10 into 10 (denominator) we cross out the 10 and put 1.

The whole multiplication process has been simplified by cancelling.

$$\dfrac{\overset{1}{\cancel{3}} \times \overset{2}{\cancel{20}}}{\underset{1}{\cancel{10}} \times \underset{11}{\cancel{33}}} = \dfrac{1 \times 2}{1 \times 11} = \dfrac{2}{11}$$

The 3, 20, 10 and 33 have disappeared, they have been cancelled down.

In summary, 3/10 x 20/33 = 60/330 = 2/11.

Example 4

More on cancelling

Multiply these	$\frac{5}{14}$	x	$\frac{7}{30}$	=	$\frac{5 \times 7}{14 \times 30}$
Two fractions					

Before we multiply the two numbers on the top line and then two numbers on the bottom.

$$\frac{5 \times 7}{14 \times 30}$$

We can see that the numbers on top & bottom are multiples of each other.

Mental Cheating

Point of order here when your kids are learning their times tables. Tell them to mentally cheat, they are kids so for some of them this should appeal to their general way of dealing with difficult tasks.

Once you have learned that $5 \times 7 = 35$

Do **NOT** stop there with one Maths questions.

    1) $5 \times 7 = 35$

    Reverse the two numbers to be multiplied.

    2) $7 \times 5 = 35$

You've now learned two for the price of one.

Say it out loud.
5, 7's are 35 then 7, 5's are 35.

    3)   Then take the answer $35 \div 5 = 7$

    4)   And then $35 \div 7 = 5$

Once you have learned 5, 7s are 35..   (5x7=35)

Then you have (by stealth) learned three others.

-       5 x 7s are 35
-       7 x 5s are 35
-       35 divided by 5 is 7
  -       And 35 divided

by 7 is 5 So back to the multiplication

$$\frac{5 \times 7}{14 \times 30}$$

Re-arrange the numerator i.e. reverse the 5 and 7.
It makes no difference 5 x 7 = 7 x 5 = 35 (as we
have just learned this trick.

$$\frac{7 \times 5}{14 \times 30} \quad = \quad \frac{35}{420}$$

Now then, 35/420 is a huge fraction and will take some simplifying.

You can see that 14 is a multiple of 7   (2 x 7 = 14)

And that 30 is a multiple of 5   (6 x 5 = 30)

We can do some cancelling.

7 will go into both 7 (once) and 14 (twice).

5 will go into both 5 (once) and 30 (six times).

(Remember ANY number divided by itself is 1).

$$\frac{{}^1 7 \times 5^1}{14_2 \times 30_6} \quad = \quad \frac{1 \times 1}{2 \times 6} \quad = \quad \frac{1}{12}$$

1/12 is the answer.

But what about if we did not cancel (simplify) and left the answer as 35/420.

Is that correct?

Yes and no.

It is a bit like how much of the pizza did you eat was it 3/6 or 1/2?

How much petrol is left in the tank of your car is it 12/16 or 3/4 ?

We have proved that 6/12 is the same as 1/2

And let us look at 12/16 we can divide both 12 and 16 by 4.

$$\frac{12}{16} = \frac{3}{4}$$

Back to 35 / 420

Can we cancel or simplify this fraction?

$$\frac{35}{420}$$

Both numerator and denominator MUST be multiples of 5 because any number ending in 5 or 0 is a multiple of 5.

We can divide both numerator (35) and denominator (420) by 5.

$$\frac{35}{420} \div \frac{5}{5} = \frac{7}{84}$$

Now we are left with 7/84.

Both 7 and 84 are multiples of 7

$$\frac{7}{84} = \frac{1}{12} \qquad \text{therefore} \quad \frac{35}{420} = \frac{7}{84} = \frac{1}{12}$$

Here are some for you to do.

$$1) \quad \frac{3}{4} \quad \times \quad \frac{5}{9}$$

$$2) \quad \frac{3}{10} \quad \times \quad \frac{5}{7}$$

1) $\dfrac{3 \times 5}{4 \times 9}$ $=$ $\dfrac{^13 \times 5}{4 \times 9_3}$ $=$ $\dfrac{1 \times 5}{4 \times 3}$ $=$ $\dfrac{5}{12}$

2) $\dfrac{3 \times 5}{10 \times 7}$ $=$ $\dfrac{3 \times 5^1}{_210 \times 7}$ $=$ $\dfrac{3 \times 1}{2 \times 7}$ $=$ $\dfrac{3}{14}$

That is how we multiply two fractions.

Simply multiply the two numerators and two denominators BUT we can make the task simpler by cancelling.

Dividing Fractions

Now here is a cute trick, we simply look at the two fractions and we perform the simple instruction called:

Stick Kiss & Flip...

Example 1

$$\frac{1}{4} \quad \div \quad \frac{9}{16}$$

The first fraction remains unchanged – we **STICK** with the 1/4 .

The divide symbol ÷ is changed and becomes a multiplication symbol x

– It becomes a **KISS**   " x ".

The second fraction is turned upside down 9/16 becomes 16/9

– We **FLIP** the 2nd fraction.

We stick with the 1/4 the ÷ becomes a x and we flip the 9/16 (Flip means turn upside down).

$$\frac{1}{4} \quad x \quad \frac{16}{9}$$

Stick   Kiss   Flip

So instead of doing a division we do a multiplication just like before.

$$\frac{1}{4} \quad x \quad \frac{16}{9} \quad = \quad \frac{1 \times 16}{4 \times 9}$$

Then we can do some cancelling.

$$\frac{1 \times 16}{4 \times 9} \quad = \quad \frac{1 \times \overset{4}{\cancel{16}}}{\underset{1}{4} \times 9} \quad = \quad \frac{1 \times 4}{1 \times 9} \quad = \quad \frac{4}{9}$$

The answer is 4 / 9

Example 2

$$\frac{2}{5} \qquad \div \qquad \frac{3}{8}$$

Stick   Kiss   Flip

$$\frac{2}{5} \qquad \times \qquad \frac{8}{3} \qquad = \qquad \frac{2 \times 8}{5 \times 3}$$

No cancelling can be done)

hen multiply top x top and bottom x bottom.

$$\frac{2 \times 8}{5 \times 3} \qquad = \qquad \frac{16}{15}$$

And we have a Top-Heavy Fraction as the answer 16/15.

Ve put bottom into top. 15 into 16 goes once (1) and 1 remainder.

Answer   =   1 and 1/15

Now I have two for you...

Questions

1) $\dfrac{2}{7}$ ÷ $\dfrac{8}{14}$

2) $\dfrac{4}{9}$ ÷ $\dfrac{10}{18}$

Answers

1) $\dfrac{2}{7} \div \dfrac{8}{14} = \dfrac{2}{7} \times \dfrac{14}{8} = \dfrac{^1 2 \times \cancel{14}^2}{^1 \cancel{7} \times \cancel{8}^4} = \dfrac{1 \times 2}{2 \times 4} = \dfrac{2}{4} = \dfrac{1}{2}$

2) $\dfrac{4}{9} \div \dfrac{10}{18} = \dfrac{4}{9} \times \dfrac{18}{10} = \dfrac{^2 4 \times \cancel{18}^2}{^1 \cancel{9} \times \cancel{10}^5} = \dfrac{2 \times 2}{1 \times 5} = \dfrac{4}{5}$

Suppose we have: - $5\frac{1}{4} \div 2\frac{1}{3}$

Mixed number 5 & ¼ divided by another mixed number 2 & ⅓

Jargon Alert:

A mixed number consists of a whole number (e.g. 5) and a fraction (e.g. ¼)

Now then we cannot easily divide mixed numbers, so we need to convert them to top heavy (improper) fractions.

So how do we convert 5¼ into a Top-Heavy Fraction

5¼   We multiply denominator (4) by the whole number (5) then add the numerator (1) and put this figure all over the old denominator (4).

$$5\frac{1}{4} \quad = \quad \frac{4 \times 5 + 1}{4} \quad = \quad \frac{21}{4}$$

Then we convert 2 1/3 into a Top-Heavy Fraction

2⅓   We multiply denominator (3) by the whole number (2) then add the numerator (1) and put this figure all over the old denominator (3).

$$2\frac{1}{3} \quad = \quad \frac{3 \times 2 + 1}{3} \quad = \quad \frac{7}{3}$$

Putting it all together

This is a GCSE style question, we deal with mixed numbers, top heavy fractions, stick, kiss, flip and throw in some cancelling.

$5 \frac{1}{4}$ $\div$ $2 \frac{1}{3}$

So that is 5 and a quarter divided by 2 and a third.

One mixed number divided by another.

Follow the six steps to find the answer: -

1)   Convert both Mixed Numbers to Top Heavy Fractions

2)   Re-write the question as one Top Heavy fraction divided by another

3)   Stick Kiss Flip

4)   Multiply the numerators / denominators

5)   Cancel (if possible)

6)   Convert back from top Heavy to a Mixed Number

Step 1

Convert both Mixed Numbers to Top Heavy Fractions 5 ¼

Start with the denominator (4) multiply by the whole number (5) then add the numerator (1) then put the answer over the denominator (4).

5 and ¼ = $\frac{21}{4}$

2 ⅓   This is then (3 x 2 + 1) all over 3

2 and ⅓ = $\frac{7}{3}$

Step 2

Re-write mixed numbers as Top-Heavy fractions.

5 ¼   ÷   2 ⅓

$\frac{21}{4}$ ÷ $\frac{7}{3}$

Step 3

$\frac{21}{4}$ ÷ $\frac{7}{3}$

Stick   Kiss   Flip

$\frac{21}{4}$ x $\frac{3}{7}$

Step 4

Multiply the numerators / denominators

$$\frac{21}{4} \quad \times \quad \frac{3}{7} \quad = \quad \frac{21 \times 3}{4 \times 7}$$

Step 5

Can we cancel any of the top numbers with the bottom numbers?

Yes, 21 is a multiple of 7.

Therefore 7 goes into 7 (once) and 7 goes into 21 (three times)

$$\frac{21 \times 3}{4 \times 7} \quad = \quad \frac{^3\cancel{21} \times 3}{4 \times \cancel{7}_1} \quad = \quad \frac{3 \times 3}{4 \times 1} \quad = \quad \frac{9}{4}$$

Step 6

Convert the Top-Heavy Fraction back into a Mixed Number

$\frac{9}{4}$ Divide Numerator (9) by the Denominator (4)
4 into 9 goes twice (2) and remainder 1.

The 2 becomes the whole number and we put the remainder (1) over the denominator (4).

$$\frac{9}{4} \quad = \quad 2 \ \& \ \frac{1}{4}$$

The Answer: $5\frac{1}{4} \div 2\frac{1}{3} = 2\frac{1}{4}$

And finally try the Stick Kiss Flip method to work these problems.

Q1:   3 and 3/4 ÷ 2 and 1/2

Q2:   5 and 4/5 divided by 2 and 2/3

Answers at the back of the book.

Conclusion

I hope you have fun reading this book even if it was the odd chapter here and there, but seriously I hope you found it useful in helping with your kids homework and getting to grips with the new methods.

And whilst I like the Multiplication Grid, Number Line, Broken Window and Stick Kiss Flip my favourite is the Chinese Box from the Shang Dynasty. I still have not worked it out how it works.

But I don't like chunking.

Anyway, I will see how well this book is received and if it goes well, I will write another one for parents with older children.

Thanks for reading Modern Maths Made Easy.

Phil Lines

Answers

Chapter 1 - Number Line

Q1: $72 - 45 = 27$

Q2: $271 - 197 = 74$

Chapter 2 - Multiplication Grid

Q1: $92 \times 65 = 5{,}980$

Q2: $82{,}458 \times 22{,}548 = 1{,}859{,}262{,}984$

Chapter 3 - Chinese Box

Q1: $38 \times 29 = 1{,}102$

Q2: $27{,}578 \times 32{,}295 = 890{,}631{,}510$

Chapter 4 - Chunking

Q1: $1400 \div 8 = 175$

Q2: $408 \div 6 = 68$

Chapter 5 - Broken Window

Q1: $3/4 + 5/7 = 41/28 = 1$ and $13/28$.

Q2: $6/7 - 2/3 = 4/21$

Chapter 6 - Stick Kiss Flip

Q1: $3\ 3/4 \div 2\ 1/2 = 15/4 \div 5/2 = 15/4 \times 2/5 = 1\frac{1}{2}$

Q2: $5\ 4/5 \div 2\ 2/3 = 87/40 = 2$ and $7/40$.

About the Author

Phil Lines graduated in Electronics Engineering in 1986 and then later took a Master's degree in Business Administration.

His life has taken many re-incarnations, Maths lecturer, training officer for a blue-chip company in London, private Maths tutor, sales manager in the field of mobile telecommunications, sales director in the family business but most importantly, a parent.

He has mentored employees and successfully taught many students to understand, enjoy and even excel at their Maths exams at various levels; 11 plus, Key Stage 3, GCSE and A level.

Many of us (including the author) would like to arrest the decline in our nation's ability to cope with the rigours of Mathematics. Phil does so, student by student, as a tutor but wants to help parents to help their children with their Maths studies which starts with helping them with their Maths homework.